stilettos in a
rifle range

Made in Michigan Writers Series

GENERAL EDITORS

Michael Delp, Interlochen Center for the Arts
M. L. Liebler, Wayne State University

A complete listing of the books in this series can be
found online at wsupress.wayne.edu.

stilettos in a rifle range

POEMS BY
TYRONE WILLIAMS

WAYNE STATE UNIVERSITY PRESS
DETROIT

Library of Congress Control Number: 2022944875

ISBN 978-0-8143-5018-8 (paperback)
ISBN 978-0-8143-5019-5 (e-book)

Publication of this book was made possible by a generous gift from The Meijer Foundation.

Cover images ©yotrak/123rf.com and ©picsfive/123rf.com. Cover design by Tracy Cox.

Wayne State University Press rests on Waawiyaataanong, also referred to as Detroit, the ancestral and contemporary homeland of the Three Fires Confederacy. These sovereign lands were granted by the Ojibwe, Odawa, Potawatomi, and Wyandot nations, in 1807, through the Treaty of Detroit. Wayne State University Press affirms Indigenous sovereignty and honors all tribes with a connection to Detroit. With our Native neighbors, the press works to advance educational equity and promote a better future for the earth and all people.

Wayne State University Press
Leonard N. Simons Building
4809 Woodward Avenue
Detroit, Michigan 48201-1309

Visit us online at wsupress.wayne.edu.

CONTENTS

vous tu

tu vous

Torched Song

p.s.

AUTHOR'S NOTE

The poems that constitute *stilettos in a rifle range* were written over a number of years while I was working on other critical and creative projects. In that sense, these "sideline" poems gave vent to other emotional and psychological states I was experiencing or recalling, living through or conjuring up, over that period of time. It so happens that I was watching and thinking about offbeat, mid- and late-twentieth century American cinema (e.g., the films of Hal Hartley) as well as, more generally, film noir. I'd become a rabid fan of the genre shortly after I moved to Cincinnati in 1983 to take an academic teaching position. After my longtime girlfriend broke up with me a month after the move, I began writing several of these poems, fueled by my sense of isolation (I knew no one in Cincinnati, hadn't met anyone aside from my colleagues at work, etc.), to say nothing of the requisite anger and frustration endemic to relationship breakups. Those poems became a part of the series titled *The Cincinnati Poems*. But as I delved deeper into film noir, I found myself fascinated with, and perplexed by, the trope of the femme fatale. Of course, it was easy to see this standard figure as simply another manifestation of the Eve-Pandora-Medea-etc. myth-as-historical model: women as intrinsically evil. This mythical/ historical legacy did not, however, square with my personal experience in relationships, including the one that had left me adrift in the new city I had to learn to call home. Plus, I'd grown up with three sisters, two of whom I was assigned to watch by my mother who, like my father, worked full time. My oldest sister, a year younger than me, and I washed dishes, changed diapers, vac-uumed floors, and fed our siblings who were nine and eleven years younger than us. In that world in which I lived—my father's mother lived with us for a while— "traditional" ideas about the roles of male and female sexes foundered when they came up against the hard practical realities of growing up in a Black working-class environment.

Don't get me wrong—these traditional patriarchal ideas were a part of the world I grew up in, and they certainly made significant inroads into the family. My father did not like the idea of my mother working full time, but he recognized, begrudgingly, that the family needed the extra income. And I certainly did not like having to wash dishes or, especially, change diapers, but whenever I started to pout or complain, the memory of those long walks to the backyard to get a switch or my father's steely look would suffice to keep my mouth shut, my thoughts and feelings securely suppressed. And just because my mother did not care about traditional gender roles when her children were pre-teens did not mean she'd discarded those ideas for good. When puberty hit me and the oldest of the sisters, the hammer came down. I got to do things, got to stay out late because, my mother explained to my confused sister, "he is a boy." And though my sister, like me, had grown up thinking girls and boys were equal because we'd had to do and share the same kinds of household responsibilities and therefore couldn't understand why our mother was suddenly and arbitrarily "changing the rules," she simply dug in her heels.

So, for me, the femme fatale figure of film noir, and Hollywood actresses in general, made sense only as an aesthetic construct, not as a model for, or representation of, actual girls and women I knew or recognized. Moreover, in the Midwest Black culture I grew up in, Black female celebrities (singers, comedians, television, and film stars, etc.) were as prominent, or at least as visible, as male ones. It is true that Black female entertainers like Moms Mabley and Pearl Bailey belonged to my parents' generation, while Black male stars seemed to dominate my own (or I only paid attention to the men). Still, a great deal of the comedy of my favorite entertainer, Richard Pryor, the Black genius of our generation, turned on both misogynist ejaculations and self-emasculating admissions, a dialectic that Pryor observed in the Midwest Black cultural and social milieu of his hometown, Peoria, Illinois. The women he slandered on stage, abused in his personal life, were, it seemed to me in my teens and early twenties, caricatures of the women in my life, though I never forgot the story of a female college friend who was followed for several miles by some guy in his car simply because she glanced at him while their cars were at a stoplight. Nor have I forgotten the moment in one of his live shows when Pryor announced that he'd decided to drop the N-word from his act, having been convinced to do so by his circle of Black entertainers and activists. By then, of course, Pryor was an international star, playing to multiracial and multiethnic audiences. But I still preferred his raw chitlin' circuit albums, the torrent of unadulterated invectives he let fly to, for, and often at his all-Black audiences. It's that unreconstructed Pryor that informs a number of the poems in this manuscript.

Still, one might wonder about the connections I drew between film noir and my experiences growing up in inner city Detroit. Certainly, class is one link; the working-class stiffs, low criminals and general ne'er-do-wells of those films could, with an instant change in race, have come directly from the streets of the Motor City I knew. And the femme fatales resembled in their behavior and attitudes the Black girls and women I grew up with and around—not only family, schoolmates, and friends but also the anonymous young Black women I observed hanging out in malls and on street corners. For example, it was only when I heard some young

Black women describing the high-heeled shoes of an apparent female friend of theirs as "fuck-me heels" that I began to draw connections between the vernaculars of film noir and young female African Americans. And like many poets, novelists, musicians, and artists to name, I recalled that the vernacular, as a vehicle for expression in folk culture, could have a powerful social force. I began to recall the "street language" of my youth in Detroit in the sixties and seventies and understood it as a "bridge" between the postwar period and the hip-hop generation. Just as some—not all—young Black women were constantly repurposing pejorative terms like *bitch*, emphasizing self-empowerment and independence (in the same way that the hip-hop generation's *nigga* was a reminder that *nigger* has different registers of value depending on the context in which it was spoken, who spoke it, and to whom it was said, none of which ended the debates about whether or not the word should ever be used . . .), so too the femme fatale has a kind of "freedom" of expression and behavior, however temporary, not available to the majority of women in a deterministic heteronormative environment.

The penultimate piece of the puzzle, so to speak, fell into place when I taught the so-called love poems of Ovid in a first-year student seminar. Before that class I hadn't read Ovid in years, but I found the range of emotions and feelings in those poems humorous, touching, and, at times, moving. Without shame I set out to emulate, as much as possible, Ovid's unsentimental takes on the sexual comedy that we dress up as "relationships" and, even more forebodingly, "love."

A final, if even more improbable, influence on the personae narrating many of these poems is the early sixties novel *DEM* by the little-known Black writer William Kelley. That work of fiction is one of the strangest and, in its own subtle way, most terrifying products of the era (Jordan Peele could learn a great deal about staging and pacing from Kelley). In the end, though, the problematic brilliance of the late comedian and actor Richard Pryor is probably the "voice" that most suffuses these poems. His humor, wit, insight, and sexism are inseparable components of what made Pryor Pryor. In thus exploring a range of attitudes, vocabularies, and emotions in these poems I want to honor the Black vernacular in all its troubled poignancy.

The Cincinnati Poems

Terre Haute

1. In Cincinnati

Dusk is the double vision of the sky—
Ranch-house high-rise scale—
This terrace that railing. Below, a valley.
We all walk off the days and nights
According to the judgment calls.
Such are the penalties of appetite.

Dusk is the double vision of the sky—
Frozen trout-mask stare of the air-drowned.
Small wonder this evening feeds so many
With so little and satisfies so few.
Down in the lowlands the hills and hospitals
Arch their backs like speed bumps.

I tour these parks, these lakes, these stray strands of your . . .

2. In Good Samaritan Hospital in Cincinnati

Charon cradles you in the craft of his arms.
Your future lies engraved in a magic writing pad.
Detroit recalls its vehicles; you, the Three Tenors.
Arias dance over your flung ashes—there,
ten o'clock, just above the IV drip.
Nothing stands between us in this limbo.
Nothing is the matter.

The dot on the retina is no longer on the screen.
Light and space shrink into ambiguous stars.
Outside the freeways shrivel into dead spiders.
The world implodes. It is you.
In the emergency room I concentrate on the tiled ceiling.
I could be floating over a floor for all I know.

3. In the Forty Thieves Restaurant in Cincinnati

The bartender barks: Hut! Hut! The bar breaks—
lumbers upstairs, a reverse-angle avalanche.
The boys ball the bitch, the bitch balls
her ass off. Bitch even takes it in the mouth.
Chokes. Fumbles. Recovers.
A fucking two-minute warning and then, over the top.

This game is won and lost on the line.

*   *   *

A Black man in a black blazer at the bar
splits his sides. White teeth flash Morse.
White shirt shivers like a flag.

4. Poolside at the New Forum Apartments in Cincinnati

A Black man baptized in black trunks.

In the blond flame of a cigarette lighter
he

disappears

reappears a

Rorschach.

5. In the Greyhound Bus Station in Cincinnati

Though your aunts in Terre Haute underwrite this Edenic mortgage, to say nothing of the service fees, Terre Haute, you say, remains your hideaway from Paradise Regained.

Between two worlds
We err—whirr—
Limbonic dancers—
Discos and dives

We shook hands, lightly brushed lips, and headed for high ground.

New York

6. In a Plane Approaching the Cincinnati Airport

On a sailboat with a father and his sons in the Catskills near Tuxedo Park I lost Terre Haute.

In a leased castle nestled on choice real estate where were the lowlands?

In the Tuxedo Inn with my ventriloquist—
speak, I heard myself, or so it seemed, say.

That valley there draws me in, down, a vortex shaped like an unstable *O*.

Detroit

7. At the Glass Menagerie in Cincinnati

At the Glass Menagerie in Covington, Kentucky
He'd just paid for his drink when a beautiful redhead
Walked up, green eyes, white teeth:
"Here's $50.00—can I suck your cock?"
Before he could close his mouth
Around the deal a Medusa-extensioned sister
Came up from behind: "I've got a century—
Can me and my girlfriend drive your car?"
When he pulled out his registration she yelled,
"You drive a Corona? That ain't even a good drink!
C'mon girl, let's get the fuck away from this broke nigger."
He glanced at the blond, her wry sneer:
"Tell you what—for a drink I'll let you lick my cunt."

8. drunken displaced detroiters

can't believe sober fridee night drink drink
up drink up home alone truss like me has u
u did talk to dem assholes fuck dem
dem complain bout shit my life sucks too
tough shit so when u cum back did way
see us gin hear low fares ah know ah know
us always cum heah we gon git out dat way
one day u mark my huh whut did u say
o thought you cid sumthin yeah cum on out
betta dan did postcard phone bullshit
shit man ah dunno I might see her might not
fuck dat bitch huh yeah u too u gots to leave
dat motherfucker u know whuh ah sayin
so how u doin cool cool yeah ahm doin okay
wait a sec gotta pee ah say peetato you say hee
hee whooooooo say u got any shrooms dey
sho do right by me and u know ah do right
ah mean it man we gon git together soon
gotta git outta did dump cincinasti u reading
anything new intrestin me just stuff for work
u know how dat shit go so whuh huh oh ahm
back on de air okay lecha go cool wait hold up—
And that ladies and gents was the new Neville
Brothers cd. Next up is Miles—a cut from *birth
of the cool*—yo man so yeah lissen
catch you latah be strong my bro okay
bye bye now don't forget to write sweetie
ta ta take care call us we love you hug hug kiss kiss

9. Somewhere in Cincinnati

High ground

        spidery lightning

The Diner (now closed)

        Patterns (now closed)

January's (now closed)

        Robin's . . . I get the picture

High ground

        watermark

credit extensions

        decompressed desire

towers east, west

        Terre Haute (closed)

Tuxedo Park (closed)

        the pool

                the strait . . .

10. Mama's Boy

for Michel Tournier, The Four Wise Men

At least once a month a man
boards a bus bound for the Motor City.
One bag, a few books. Nevertheless,
he always tells himself
I just might leave Cincinnati for good—
just cut out—
never look back . . .

When he arrives in Detroit he drinks
and drinks it all in until he's dead drunk
on all fours, a two-year-old
mama's boy, bawling
all night, night after night
for the salty milk of his mother
turning in her sleep from a hard back . . .

When he takes at long last
the last bus back to the Queen City,
long after the only rest stop,
he notices the first signs:
merciless thirst, swollen ankles,
what the folks down South
call sugar.

stilettos in a rifle range

Imperfect Angel

for Minnie Riperton

When her sunward singing started waning as she surged starward

and
fell
fading
shrieks
piercing
moot
octaves

the thunderclap of her body turning water into wine
broke the earth
                          like bread

vous tu

Random Late-Night Calls

O the awkward equations of errant attachments!
O voluptuous multiple ovals aloom!
Virally exact, a virtual face-to-face
cloaks the fiber-optic kiss-and-tell.
I open to the coo of "hoo dis?"
Dear Stranger—how are you this evening?

Yes, the chickens wobble—or plummet—coopward—
Yes, I know only "we" can read the bones—
See, she ripples the veil of never-was.
Off-screen the chorus giggles itself to shush.
She prattles on about. I want to do
that, that—and especially that—to her.

If one of her girlfriends can babysit.
If I can get to the 24/7 drugstore.
If we can hit a Denny's later.
Soon, soon. In which key *is* the whisper?
We drone like radios tuned to the bottom of the dial.
The margin is just another toolbox.

H-Bomb

Her fuck-me heels will have been heard, hers
                    will have should, should
                    a deep throat
striangulated by the hands of a clockety-stop
                    a pretty watched
                    ticked-tocked-
off the fuck-you effect of Doppergangbusters.

like something cute was about to start

Jean Harlow, Bombshell

The way the ass of the world—
abacus absent ball bearings—
sumptuous in the innie of cupped

squeezees squeaky-high do
it B-10 style

points tit for tat

How M. L. Beavers milk honey-
(neither gypped nor jewed)
comb kinks cock-

[high Hattie Mc-
walk-the-sheep-]

a-doodle-*Red Dust* rag

-dogs sans TGIF sheep—
talkies-silenced silents—
but for the butt

-too force-fed for two-
piece bikini atoll

glass of tease=two fingers

Belle Isle, Detroit

lungs parked alongside lungs
lungs taking in the CO_2 of inside jobs

heads in laps
lap all m

orality
pulls ahead

flung back
en ec-

tap that app
slap slap

bottoms ump
       ump

armspan on legs akimbo
Trojan horse brainstemville

Damn!

Quickie nibble
Pop-up nipple

Butter is the new
Thumbs up a fine piece

Dot *t* & *a*
Cross-eyed *n*

Reading Ohio

A former border town now a
    township

stamped upon a tall glass of speed
    trap

poured roll through a penta-
    STOP—

    she's gone—

insipid lyric with a little English
    on it—

backspin to the finished basement
    on Burns

St. where I brushed against a still
    wet

like day and night

A formal leggy acid
pours out of a lemon

touted as a big banana.
The smile of zero

gravity draws flash
crowds unstrings the moon

so over.

Legpecker

One whale
     of a right gam
          slung over
       a left knee
            swings
back   and   forth
like   a   backyard   swing
                    toe-tapping a right
                           shimmy
                                shin
                                shin

The Don't-Note

A flourish of half
fortissimo for the whole—
suspended—he-bang.

Baby, Ba-bay

No sliding, much
        less, slurring,
long *e* don't even get the short end,
        all *a* all the
washing out *b* with its back-
        water *y* dry
as a whistle about to be blown.

tu vous

A Blind of Thumbs

Her hands were not hers
to hand out, much less
to herself, least of all

to the lower case
of a third back, unarched,
if anything, the opposite,

however offhandedly,
a first person, singular,
if not single, leaning

back into her, my,
if not mine, hand
behind the back

legs of a chair,
or two, hands crossed hands
set, at best, to clap,

worst, pat (however passed
the point of clasp), near impossi—
no—opposa—ble backs.

Unentitled

A dark hand over a dark hand
equals

minus
everything except x

Spoon

Sitting next to you
I place my right palm
       over your
       left knuckles
squeeze

Slightly   and only
              once, a
single handbeat for
unspoken writing.

And the Spell Was Broken

And then your sister
And then your niece and brother
Walked back into the room.

Filigustibuster

Oh my oh
Must be really
You simply must
Hmmmnnn that *is*
Isn't it the
Yes. Would you
Just a little
Okay . . . How's
Really good
Glad you. Would
No thanks I'm
Well then how
Uh no I
Not even a
No but thank
You can sip
You already had
Think of it
What. A Roman
Sure. You just
That's gross
Look. The alcohol
I don't I'm
All right Sorry
What's the big
No big just
What You what
I just thought
Backdoor me
I guess you could
Kissing cup. Right.

Tsariana

Another cognate in an alphabet,
Warped after a long tenure in the waters,
I, T, stand mute before S
while she runs on and on, gabbing after
every letter A to R. Nothing
more than a common tart
(I would lower myself to, to double-cross
the little slut by sleeping with her nonidentical twin,
Z), S, mirror of many
nonesuch discourses, lists, tilts,
a slit—ankle to vulva—in a
skirt black as sails . . .

Dear R, Dear S

s'il vous plait
respondez- [rendez-, perhaps,
with either vous, mes petites,
or just tu. . . .]
                        The party I threw
(just pour deux)
                                    is almost over
                        my sad balloons, sagging,
the streamers, wrinkled, crinkled,
                        and the guests—
my dearly departed, my beard—have left
                        me ici,
ice melting in hands, palms,
                        turned up,
dogs on their backs.

As

Hands in heaven
I pull the string on S:

"Sorry to bother you again, R,
but have you seen T?"

In Whom I Am

Because whatever she was saying she was sure
fell short
I heard her palm alight on my arm.

A thicket of ashes I caught myself
listening to a glint—
the blade I raised as if my own arm.

Connipniption

Shakeyourmindviolentlylikesome hologram initscribbraindead

Don't Lean on the Horn

Slow down, slow down—you're not Cary Grant.

Slow down—the food's not going anywhere.

Wait, wait—go back a few channels.

Slow down—do you have to tailgate?

Slow down—do you have to walk ahead of me?

Wait—slow down—you just ran over a bunch of roses.

What do you mean you already came?

Go,

Hurry up.

Get the hell out.

Wounded, Dead

He find hisself
kicked to the curb, she
flung up a flight of stairs where I
—clothesline—
—trip wire—
cut the crust from that slice of pie.

She, her,

that disturbance outside—
exegetes-cum-peeping-toms
stumbling through the flowerbeds.
Won't raise the blinds, cry uncle,

pimp the pronouns
standing guard
on either side

of this sentence-
prison cell-
sanctuary-

confessional
box where Turing
hyphens and duple

bars gossip
in one eave
and out the other

   drop earmarked
for a proper
nounnery.

Extinct: Male

When she came she came too—come-cum-come—teething urinals bookending the blank sheets of the hallowed monitors.

PRND

A downpour drumming on the rooftop,
engine running, car, idle, interior
bathed in the pungent intoxicating spices
radiating from the carryout
in the passenger seat. Inside the Taj,
neon beacon in a strip mall
dark with the common sense of folks
long gone home, red lamps
glowered. A pair of headlights
glared back. A downpour drowning
out its own drumming, so loud
I could barely make out the whispered venom
streaming from a mobile into my right ear.
She was saying something about something
as I reached across the steering column
with my left hand, as if my left ear
had been bent by the loudspeaker of the law.
Engine off, everything—the car, the carryout, etc.—
went cold. I tossed the phone into the passenger seat,
put her into reverse, backed up, out,
and drove home with my double order,
her running commentary as undertow.

Toys Were Us

Dear Barbie, you fuck,
you got your Ken, the doll house,
    the two kids, thanks to
his ex, that white hell-on-heels
you hate, miss chocolate snowflake.

*   *   *

Dear wannabe Ken-
nigger, please, nobody wants
to hear your piss-poor ass
pout. Having some—wish you were
here to trim the hedges, hoss.

Antigonistes

(AP) Bitch on the loose—
or prowl. Repeat: impera-
tive flees indicative. That
is, the set of all sets rears
up—Set. Armed with sash
—check: rope—check: n-
ooze—check: leaking ex-
treme necktie. Alert: poon-
tang on the lam. Z tombie.
Too late to talk, table the
periodic, but can that sister
bring her in from the cold?
Can't believe this disbelief
—cunt cut out.

This report
was filed by Creon, second father, first son, with special assistance from the net.

Blue Blues

Bigger little
boy blue
head to head—

shy, sleight,
or a slight
tug of the skirt

south, if not south
of blue knees—
or a slight exaggeration—

quite, such,
a pill. Blue is how I roll
bottoms up

Enjambment Avalanche

Pumping iron lotions rusty elbows
"and ten low words oft creep in one dull line"

Dusty barbells rat me out,
ashy knees I try to play off,

but misdirection is a boomerang–
yo-yo combo meal the quarterback

has to eat. Helmet in hand, I head off
the field to ride the bench, to ride it out,

all of which means I miss you less
than I did the day you dropped a rhyming

couplet—goodbye/ty—followed by
a single whole rest note you still sustain . . .

A Weekend Away

I have never slept as well as I did that first evening,

the cottage rental
bay windows
open to the breezy amenities of Lake Superior

lazy walks
bicycle rides
and a picnic

       peppered with profanities, shouts,
the afterglow of rage.

An umbrella of smog sheltered the city swelling on the horizon, a standing army of randomly assorted pawns, queens, and kings. We were almost home and our only hope was that the other would die, just fucking die.

Boo

O my
x-mine
corpse forlorned
exhumed
tomb
is a haunted house
degilded room
in which
what goes
who ghosts
me in
my O

you

free

fall

Tapeworm

I am listing on indivisible seas . . .

I can taste the sirens in the background . . .

that voice that once destroyed the world and cruelly resurrected it once and for all that voice that sentenced me to life and roughly shook the foil awake with low probability of rain that voice unearthed rises from and through a buried alive half-

anima ex machina

Torched Song

A Smile

wide as the slumbering tsunamis between us

is a kiss
asunder

sa-gil
pout

black angel hair over brown shoulder blade, rare

cut

soft decapitation—half treading earthquakes

As If

Lady, your back-breaking fingers so carefully manhandle jet hair . . .

Hong Kong Song

Behind your Hong
Kong to Kong
pidgin-told
tale I gets
twice an eye
for fine China

* * *

                    When I penned your letters
                    to my stereotypewriter
                    way out fronting handwriting

* * *

Now not-our cell to cell
calls when all wont to do is text
            or sext
            u up

* * *

                    Later, let's baby the next
                          Generation X-
                          pad, pat

* * *

Fuck me?
Count those upside-down french fries hanging out your bag.
Nails drying while I'm driving nails—fuck that, baby
                    baby, baby
                    baby

How on Earth

The klutz of Tao
tumbleweeds

past, kaput
flaneur, Janus-

kneecaps
wrecked akimbo—

all points
Buddha and Buda-

pest, she-
wolf whistle

and all ears,
paws, and drool

he come a—
not e—loping,

nose open
wide to that wanton

wisp, his pungent
errantress.

Not Entitled

A funeral pyre of white roses, red buds, seedless grapes, veils, throws . . .

Olde

Your
laughter is the song that parts your lips
karaoke
singing violins
praise-cum-joy-spangled banners
icing the cake and ice
cream tongue-numb cold

laughter is a sea crossing the ocean
yours

The Hair Lady

walks between her waterfalls wetless as the shade
        they offer as their
shadows flickering across the wall of a cliff

walks as and as among and wonders of the world
        where and when will rain
wide and long enough to waken the sleeping sun-
        flowers everywhere

        but here and there fall
like the hair she cannot do anything with but
        yank from her bowed head.

The Fifth World

A terrible two washes ashore, driftwood among the mangrove ghosts.

Unclasped

Your fingers bend the wrong way, weeping willows dragged skyward by the hair . . .

The Vennus Virus

In an envelope
slipped into the side pocket—
flanked by the legal

pad-handler of a frontispiece leather-bound
file folder at the back of a cabinet
framed by the furniture of folding
"work" into "area" in a house in

a city, a world,
etcetera . . . absolute
universe—a hand,
severed from its wrist as clean-
ly as the nothing between

it and other hands, remains "in
it" as remains of a fleeting
grasp, heavenly asteroid
inflated into an envoi,
cornered stamp. In an envelope
rough salt, leftover from your

tongue, absorbs the last drops of moisture
from the cut roses enclosed. An
avocado-yellow piece
of cheap string promoted
to crinkled sash, poised
to distribute
affective

orders, holds a piece of card-
board (folded into a card)
down, if not downsized, the card
lunging forth like a wild Can-
tonese from a throat concealed
by a Mandarin mouth. Ciao,
in effect: an envelope
of tropes flash cards the occult.

Wah Wah

Pigeon-Englished
we milk this mix: wild
lisps: malapropos lips
     guffaw fingers
loitering palms—some
     pidgin-toed quadruped
in a moot boudoir—
     sunflower pink—pawed
savanna, sheer
     drop of a black waterfall
splashing pools of awww . . .

Wahku

Broken almost in
    two we fell away and in—
        crushed *U*: Handsmade *V*.

p.s.

stilettos in a rifle range

She and she
said switch
so swish

        he did, having misheard,
        heard, he slid into a pair
        of, slipped into an, open-

back heels and dress,
they, following suit,
she, his jacket, shirt,

        she, his pants, wingtips,
        tearing down the set
        pieces, flipped the dinner

party, a three-ring
au pair a trois
staging the blank glint

        mute smirk,
        wine glasses
        half raised, lowered

to half-staff,
flagging something
in the airs,

        chi chi noses
        wrinkled with
        the stiff whiff

of a flat mistake
aquiline for Roman
knock-off

        defanged the gang:
        "It was all a gag,"
        they cried, laughed.

Trauungschrift

enhorabuena a la feliz pareja

خوش جوڑے کو مبارک ہو

সুখী দম্পতি করতে অভিনন্দন

oriire si ku tọkọtaya

מאַזל—טאָוו צו די גליקלעך פּאָר

ahniah kepada pasangan bahagia

Congratulazioni alla coppia felice

מזל טוב לזוג המאושר

Parabéns para a parella feliz

gratuluji k šťastnému páru

enhorabona a la feliç parella

تهانينا للزوجين سعيدة

llongyfarchiadau i'r cwpl hapus

تهانينا للزوجين سعيدة

Mutlu çift tebrikler

Поздравляем счастливую пару

gratulacje dla szczęśliwej pary

gratulatione ad beatum duorum

幸せなカップルにおめでとう

συγχαρητήρια για το ευτυχισμένο ζευγάρι

õnnitlused õnnelik paar

祝賀幸福的情侶

віншуем шчаслівае пару

Felisitasyon koup la kè kontan

CREDITS

"Terre Haute," "Housed and Homeless," "At January's," "drunken displaced Detroiters," and "Mama's Boy" in *Brooding the Heartlands: Poets of the Midwest*. Bottom Dog Press, 1998, 139–47.

"Like something cute was about to start," *P-QUEUE*, vol. 6 (2009): 9.

"The Vennus Virus," *OmniVerse* 17 (Summer 2012).

"How on Earth," *Post Road* 25 (2013): 99.

"Wah Wah," *Post Road* 25 (2013): 100.

"Antigonistes," *Eleven Eleven*.

"Imperfect Angel," *Chicago Review* 62:4/63:1/2 (Fall/Winter 2019), 370.

"Hong Kong Song," "Belle Isle" and "Baby, Bab-ay," *Marsh Hawk Review*.